The IMMA~~CULATE~~
CONCEPTION

PATRONESS OF THE AMERICAS

REV. JUDE WINKLER, OFM Conv.

Imprimi Potest: Mark Curesky, OFM Conv., Minister Provincial of St. Anthony of Padua Province (USA)
Nihil Obstat: Francis J. McAree, S.T.D., Censor Librorum
Imprimatur: ✠ Patrick J. Sheridan, D.D., Vicar General, Archdiocese of New York

The Nihil Obstat and Imprimatur are official declarations that a book or pamphlet is free of doctrinal or moral error. No implication is contained therein that those who have granted the Nihil Obstat and Imprimatur agree with the contents, opinions or statements expressed.

GOD CREATES THE WORLD

IN the beginning God created the heavens and the earth and everything that is in them. God created all of these things because He wanted to share the great love that the Father had for the Son and the Holy Spirit and that the Son and the Spirit had for the Father and each other. All that God created was filled with that love.

God created the sun and the moon and the stars in the sky. He created the birds of the air and the fish in the sea. He created cows and sheep and cats and dogs.

Every time that God created something, He saw how good it was. He was filled with joy, because all of these things were so good.

But the thing that brought God the most joy was the man and the woman whom He created. He created the first man who was named Adam and the first woman who was named Eve.

He created them with so much love that they even resembled God. The Bible tells us that God created them in His image and His likeness. They were the best of everything that God had made, and God was very pleased with what He had done.

THE FIRST SIN

GOD planted a garden for Adam and Eve in a place called Eden. He cared for them, and they would walk with God in the garden every evening.

God told Adam and Eve that they could eat the fruit of any of the trees in the Garden of Eden except for one tree. They were not to eat the fruit of the tree of knowledge of good and evil.

One day Satan appeared to Eve in the form of a snake. Satan tempted Eve to eat of the tree of the knowledge of good and evil. He told her that the only reason that God did not want her to eat of that tree was because God did not want Adam and Eve to become like Him.

Eve listened to the lies of the snake and she was greatly tempted. She took some of the fruit from the tree and ate it. She also gave some to Adam and he ate it.

As soon as they ate the fruit, they realized they had done something very bad. They had sinned against God's love. They felt guilty, and when God came to walk with them in the garden, they hid themselves. They were ashamed because they were not wearing any clothes.

THE PUNISHMENT FOR SIN

GOD called Adam and Eve and asked them why they were hiding themselves. Adam answered that he was afraid for he was naked. God knew that Adam and Eve had done what He told them not to do. He told them that they had done something very wrong and that they must be punished.

God told Adam that he would work very hard but never really succeed in what he was doing. He then told Eve that she would have great pain when she would have a child.

Finally, He told the snake that it would be punished for tempting Adam and Eve. It would lose its legs and have to crawl about on the ground.

Yet God still loved Adam and Eve. He did not want to punish them forever. He promised them that One would be born who would crush the head of the snake. This was a promise that God would send One who would destroy the power of sin.

God also made clothes for Adam and Eve. He sent them forth from the Garden of Eden to wander upon the earth.

ORIGINAL SIN

THIS first sin was very bad, for God had shown so much love to Adam and Eve and they had turned their backs on His love.

This sin left Adam and Eve much weaker, for every time that someone sins, it is easier for that person to sin in the future. For example, once I tell one lie, it is easier to lie to other people. Or if I steal something small, it becomes easier to steal something large. Adam and Eve were badly hurt by their sin.

Their children also suffered from the sin of Adam and Eve. Even before the children were born, they were hurt by sin. From their very first moment of life, they suffered from the effects of that first sin. We call this original sin.

All of us who are born suffer from the effects of original sin. It is so easy for us to do what is wrong. It is so easy for us to turn our backs on God's love.

This sin grew worse and worse in the world. Once God even decided to punish the world for its sin by sending a great flood. He saved only Noah and his family from the flood, but even then people continued to sin.

9

SALVATION HISTORY

YET God would not abandon His people. He called Abraham and Sarah to become the father and mother of His people. He promised that they would become a great nation and He would be their God and they would be His people.

He rescued His people from slavery in Egypt through his holy servant Moses. He gave Moses the two tablets upon which He had written the Law for His people: the Ten Commandments.

God called forth holy men and women to lead His holy people. He called people like Deborah to be a judge over His people, and David to be a great king.

He sent great Prophets to speak to His people and call them to live according to His Law. There were Prophets like Isaiah and Jeremiah who taught the people how much God loved them and how they should love Him in return.

But no matter how many times God called His people through their leaders and Prophets and priests, they always turned back to their sin. Adam and Eve's sin had so weakened the people that they could not find the strength to be faithful to God's call.

THE IMMACULATE CONCEPTION

THAT is why God chose to send His only Son into the world. Jesus was the only One Who could free us from our slavery to sin. Without His help, we would never have been able to respond to God's call with love.

God had prepared for the arrival of His Son by sending Prophets to call His people back to the ways of the Lord. They all spoke of that day when God's justice would change our world.

God also prepared for the birth of His Son in a very special way. He wanted the Mother of His Son to be completely filled with love. Yet, all of us were wounded by original sin, and we do not know how to love as we should. So God protected Mary, the daughter of Joachim and Ann, from original sin. She would become the Mother of His Son.

We call this miracle the Immaculate Conception. From the very first moment of her life, Mary was protected from the pain of sin and its effects. And Mary responded to this miracle of love. Unlike Adam and Eve who had rejected God's love through sin, Mary always responded to God's call with great generosity. She never sinned throughout her entire life.

THE ANNUNCIATION AND VISITATION

THEN, one day, God sent an angel named Gabriel to Nazareth in order to speak to Mary. The angel greeted Mary saying, "Hail, Mary, full of grace; the Lord is with you." By greeting her this way, the angel was saying that Mary was a very special person. She was completely filled with God's love.

Gabriel then asked Mary if she would become the Mother of the Son of God. Mary responded to God's call by saying, "I am the servant of the Lord. Be it done unto me according to your word." Mary was saying that she was willing to do whatever God wanted of her. She was a very generous person, and all she wanted to do was to help others.

We see that from what she did next. She went to visit her cousin Elizabeth who needed her help. Elizabeth was the mother of John the Baptist, and she was very old, so she needed Mary's help until her child was born.

Elizabeth greeted Mary saying, "Who am I that the mother of my Lord should come to me." Elizabeth knew that Mary's baby would be very special, for the minute she saw her, the baby in her womb, John the Baptist, jumped for joy.

MARY, THE MOTHER OF JESUS

WHEN it came time for Mary to have her baby, she and Joseph traveled to Bethlehem. They stayed in a cave where the animals were kept, for there was no room in the inn.

Great signs were seen when her son, Jesus, was born. Angels sang in the sky. Shepherds and Magi traveled to pay homage to the child. All were amazed at the greatness of God's love.

Joseph and Mary and Jesus had to flee to Egypt to save Jesus from king Herod. Later, they went to Nazareth where Jesus grew in strength and wisdom. When Jesus was twelve, He was lost in the temple for three days. When Mary and Joseph found Him, He told them that He had to be about His Father's business.

Mary cared for Jesus until He began His Public Ministry when He was about thirty years old. From then on, she prayed for Him in a special way and was with her Son only at times. She was there that horrible day when Jesus died on the Cross. Before He died, Jesus entrusted Mary to the beloved disciple. From that day on, he cared for her. Mary was also with the disciples when the Holy Spirit descended on the first Pentecost Sunday.

DEVOTION TO MARY

WHEN Mary's life on earth was ended, God continued the miracle of His love for her and her love for Him. He brought her into heaven body and soul. We call this her Assumption.

Very soon after this time, people began to pray to Mary. She was a perfect example of what it meant to be a Christian, and they asked for her help in order to respond to God's call.

One of the earliest prayers to her states, "We take refuge under the protection of your motherly mercy, O Mother of God. Deliver us from danger. Rescue us. You alone are the Pure One. You alone the Blessed one."

All throughout the centuries, devotion to Mary, the Mother of God, has grown. Many of the great cathedrals built during the Middle Ages were dedicated to her protection. Many great preachers spoke of how we should seek Mary's help and follow her example.

One of these great teachers, a man named Blessed John Duns Scotus, spoke about Mary. He was one of the first to teach that God had favored Mary from the first moment of her life for she was truly the Immaculate Conception.

MARY AND THE AMERICAS

WHEN Columbus and the first people from Europe arrived in the Americas in 1492, they brought with them a special devotion to Mary. One of Columbus' ships, in fact, was named the Santa Maria, which means St. Mary. Soon after their arrival, in 1531, Mary appeared in a vision called Our Lady of Guadalupe.

An Indian named Juan Diego was on his way to Mass when he heard beautiful music. He looked up and saw a light on a hill and standing there was a beautiful young woman. She spoke to him in his native language and asked that a church be built on that spot to honor her.

Juan Diego went to the bishop, who asked for some sign as proof of what he had said. Mary sent a powerful sign to the bishop. She had Juan Diego gather some roses that were growing on the hill (even though it was winter). He placed them in his mantle and carried them to the bishop. When he emptied his mantle, there was a beautiful image of Mary on it.

The bishop wept when he saw this great miracle. He ordered that a great basilica be built. Our Lady of Guadalupe is revered to this day, and we celebrate her feast on December 12.

THE EARLY SETTLERS AND MARY

OTHER explorers and settlers brought devotion to the Americas as well. The Spanish explorer Martinez founded the city of St. Augustine in Florida, the oldest city in the United States. The day he founded it, he had a Mass celebrated in honor of the Nativity of Our Lady. Likewise, the city of Los Angeles is really named after Mary, the Queen of the Angels. The French explorer of the Mississippi River, Father Marquette, named that river, "the River of the Immaculate."

In most of the English colonies, there was little devotion to Mary. The reason for this was that Catholics were not allowed to settle in most of the colonies, and they were often persecuted if they traveled there.

The exceptions to this were two colonies: Pennsylvania and Maryland. Pennsylvania was founded by the Quakers, and they allowed people of any faith to settle there.

Maryland, on the other hand, was settled by Catholics. It was to be a safe haven for Catholics who had been persecuted for their faith in England. The Catholics who landed there founded a city named after Mary: St. Mary's, Maryland.

PATRONESS OF THE UNITED STATES

THE first diocese in the United States was founded in 1790. The first bishop of the diocese of Baltimore, which at that time included all of the United States, was John Carroll. He dedicated his diocese to the protection of the Blessed Virgin Mary.

As the number of Catholics grew in America, more and more dioceses were founded. Many of them dedicated themselves to the protection of our Lady. The first cathedral in the United States was begun in Baltimore in 1806 and it, too, was dedicated to our Lady.

Then, in 1846, the bishops of the young country of the United States of America gathered in Baltimore. They asked the Holy Father for permission to dedicate the United States to our Lady under the title of the Immaculate Conception.

A few years later, in 1854, the Holy Father, Pope Pius IX, declared that the Immaculate Conception was a dogma of the Church. This means that all Catholics must believe that God truly did preserve Mary from the effects of the original sin. We celebrate the Feast of the Immaculate Conception on December 8.

26

I AM THE IMMACULATE CONCEPTION

ON February 11, 1858, our Lady appeared to a fourteen-year-old peasant girl named Bernadette in Lourdes, France. Mary appeared to her eighteen times over the next several months.

Mary's message was very simple. She told her, "Pray to God for sinners" and "Do penance," to bring people closer to the Lord.

On March 25, Mary revealed to Bernadette that she was the Immaculate Conception. Bernadette was not educated, and she did not even know the meaning of this revelation, but this was the truth that Pope Pius IX had declared to be a dogma of the faith four years before.

As at Guadalupe, Mary sent a sign to show that this revelation was from God. She told Bernadette to dig a hole in the ground. Bernadette obeyed and found a spring that gives about 25,000 gallons of water a day.

Many people have traveled to Lourdes, where a great basilica has been built over the site of Mary's apparition. Many people who were sick have been healed there. Bernadette was canonized as a saint in 1933. We celebrate the feast of Our Lady of Lourdes on February 11.

GREATER HONOR TO MARY

IN the United States, it was proposed in 1913 that a national shrine should be built in Washington D.C. dedicated to our Lady, the Immaculate Conception. The basilica was begun in 1931 and the Church was dedicated in 1959. Thousands of people travel to Washington every year as pilgrims to ask for the intercession of Mary.

There have been other movements as well to further devotion to Mary throughout the world. In 1921, a great Marian movement called the Legion of Mary was founded in Ireland.

Another movement dedicated to Mary was founded in Rome in 1919 by St. Maximilian Kolbe. This movement is called the Militia of the Immaculate. St. Maximilian Kolbe believed in using the most modern means to proclaim our faith to the world. He printed magazines and newspapers. He even founded a radio station.

During World War II, he was arrested by the Nazis and taken to a concentration camp. There he saw a man being dragged off to his death, crying out that he would never see his wife or children again. Fr. Kolbe offered himself in place of that man, and he died in the camp on August 14, the day before the feast of the Assumption.

THE IMMACULATE CONCEPTION TODAY

DEVOTION to Mary, the Immaculate Conception, is a devotion that we need today more than ever. There is so much violence in our world. Many people live selfish lives. Mary gives us an example of someone who dedicated herself totally to the service of God and others.

Our families often suffer from many difficulties. Many children grow up without a father or a mother. Mary, the Immaculate Conception, is a Mother for all of us. Even if our own parents cannot always love us with a perfect love, she can. And so Mary, the Immaculate Conception, offers to hold us in her arms as a loving Mother.

Mary also points to the truth that Jesus should be the center of our lives. Whenever she has appeared in a vision, she has called people to turn back to the Lord. She calls us to prayer and fasting so that we can turn back from our sins.

Finally, we pray to Mary, the Immaculate Conception as the patroness of our country. The United States was established as one nation under God. We must find a way to live as a people who give witness to God's love. We must be as generous with our service and the blessings we have received as Mary was.

PRAYERS TO MARY IMMACULATE

O Mary, conceived without sin,
pray for us who have recourse to you,
and for those who do not have recourse to you,
especially the enemies of the Church
and those who are most in need of your mercy.
  Amen.

———

O Mary,
you entered the world without stain of sin.
Obtain for me from God
that I may leave it without sin. Amen.